A Celebration of Winter

DAVID ADAM

'A man who has lost his sense of wonder is a man dead.'

William of Thierry (1085–1148)

Published in Great Britain in 2006

Society for Promoting Christian Knowledge
36 Causton Street
London SW1P 4ST

British Library Cataloguing-in-Publication Data
A catalogue record for this book is available from the British Library.

ISBN-13: 978-0-281-05715-3
ISBN-10: 0-281-05715-X

1 3 5 7 9 10 8 6 4 2

Designed and typeset by Monica Capoferri
Printed in China by Compass Press Ltd

INTRODUCTION

To celebrate winter we need to have child-like hearts and minds. To enjoy this season it is important that we retain a sense of wonder and awe of what is around us. We should be able to thrill at the first snows and admire a single snowflake or, from the comfort of a room, gaze at the frost patterns on the window that are full of mystery, and let them lift the heart. We will not think for a moment of the dangers of travelling, the traffic chaos or the increasing cold. Instead, we will rejoice to walk in virgin snow, and delight in making footprints or following the tracks of hare, rabbit or deer, while hoping to glimpse them. The paw prints of a dog may be imagined to be those of a fox or wolf as we enter into a spirit of adventure in a transformed world.

Winter is a time to appreciate the security of home and to curl up in its comfort and warmth. We might not hibernate, but this season is a time to relax before the fire with friends or with a good book. Winter is often a challenge to change our routines and to accept that we live in a world that is forever changing. There will be some days at least when we have to admit that our normal patterns will not work. Then we can allow frustration to hold sway and moan or we can celebrate a change in routine and a life that is neither entirely predictable nor fully under control.

Children get excited as sledges come out of sheds and from hidden places. The long trudge uphill will be amply rewarded by the freedom of flying down the hill at speed. A few spills are part of the fun and the excitement of the experience. It does not matter that it takes only seconds to come down and minutes to walk uphill: both are part of the adventure in a world painted white. Cold hands, ears and feet are ignored as snowballs are made and snow sculptures formed. This is often a time for family members to enjoy the experience together, to celebrate the delight they have in one another's company and the fun they share.

Winter has been chosen as the time to celebrate the coming of God and the birth of Jesus. In the dark days, we can applaud the fact that light is stronger than darkness and brighter days are to come. Christmas is very close to the shortest day when darkness seems to have got the upper hand. Yet, because of Christ's coming down, the darkness is conquered. It is a time to light candles, to decorate our homes and welcome the Lord of Light.

Our world has so often lost its ability to celebrate. The festivals have become bland or remote from us. Laurens Van der Post describes people as 'festival hungry'. To rejoice fully, we need to breathe new life into our celebrations, to look with new eyes at Advent, Christmas and Epiphany; and, if we do not know them, to enjoy the adventure of going down these ways. It is a great joy when our lives overflow with a sense of occasion that we want to mark and to share with others. We need to create some festivals of our own and show that life is to be revelled in with wonder and with joy. Such celebration can help in giving meaning and purpose to our lives.

Come join with me and celebrate winter: celebrate life.

THE COMING OF WINTER

A northerly wind hardens the ground
Turning pools and ponds solid
And halting the stream in its course
The dripping tap turns into a spear
Patterns appear on the window
And the grass is glazed with the frost
The robin comes to feed by hand
The blackbirds venture close
But the little wren keeps well way
Breath streams from every mouth
Hands tingle, feet feel icy cold
Now we know – winter is here

SNOWFLAKES

We are stars come from heaven
Six-pointed and virgin white
High above you were we born
Crystallized and rare in making
Flowers preparing to come to earth
Each one individual
And wonderfully unique
Yet we come in millions
Softly and without a sound
To transform the brown earth
To paint hill, town and tree
To delight the children
And all who have eyes to see

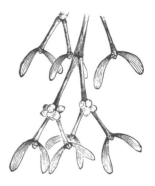

CELEBRATING ADVENT

Advent has within it the longest night of the year and the darkest days. It is easy to let the gloom enter our lives and our whole being. Yet we can choose to celebrate these four weeks before Christmas, illuminating our homes and filling our lives with hope. Advent is meant to celebrate the coming of God and so should be a season of joy and light.

Think about the saying 'It is better to light one small candle than to complain about the darkness.' Then decide to brighten each day with the awareness that God comes to you. God has never left his world. He is with you even on the darkest days. God comes to you as he came in the days of old. Because God came especially in Jesus Christ, I light candles throughout Advent to affirm that in Jesus, the Light of the World, the darkness is dispersed and even death is conquered.

Take a small plate and place on it four night-lights with a fifth in the centre. Now put it in a place that you choose for your time of quiet. The first week light only one candle, the second week two and so on until the four outer ones are lit. This way, as the days darken, you affirm that the light of Christ is stronger than any darkness – and that Christ comes to you. Light all five candles on Christmas day to celebrate that Christ is born. Make this a family celebration if you can. Begin with a short silence. Let someone light the candle and say: 'God loves us and comes to us.' Then invite God into your life and say:

'Come, Lord God, lighten our darkness
Come, Lord God, fill us with your love
Come, Lord God, keep us in your peace
Come, Lord God, be known among us
Come, Lord God.'

If you are not saying this alone, let the words 'Come, Lord God' be said by all.

THE BARN OWL

Not a sound as it passes by
A spectre gliding over the fields
Weaving among the snowflakes
Wings in regular rhythm

Then in a moment it has vanished
A white phantom of the night
Conjured up by the mind
Something of the spirit only

Was it really there at all?
Or just a passing dream?
Suddenly, a plaintive call –
A barn owl in the snow

WINTER SENSATIONS

Look at the whiteness all around
Trace the patterns of frost on glass
Crunch through the snow upon the ground
Feel the sharp chill in the air
Hear the sighing of the wind
Listen as carols are joyfully sung
Smell the pine trees on the breeze
Inhale the smoky-scented air
Taste the newly made mince pies
Savour all the Christmas fare
Relax before a fire, at ease –
Come and celebrate each of these!

CAROLS ACROSS THE DALES

The music drifts over snow-filled dales
The song of moorland folk and angels
Choristers with lanterns on shepherds' crooks
Trudge through snow and drift
And fields aglitter with frosty stars
Serenading lonely farmhouse after farmhouse
With old tunes and carols sweet:
'Peace on earth, good will to all people.'
Doors stand open and welcome
There's a hot toddy to encourage the singing
A mince pie to bless yet another year
Cheeks glow briefly in the warmth
Before the song calls and bids us take our leave

Ah, how many Decembers since then?
So many have moved away
Some we would never meet again
Others returned to kiss under the mistletoe
Every winter, long sung carols fill the air
For life and its music travel on

THE TRUE CHRISTMAS

The ingredients for Christmas are simplicity and mystery. Without some simplicity, we lose the value of the small thing and, without the mystery, we cannot approach the wonderful events remembered in this season. Within all our activity and our celebrations, we need to make space for simplicity and for mystery. The true Christmas balances the two.

It was right that the first Christmas was of the greatest simplicity. There was no beautiful room or fancy clothing, only the basics of life. A stable, a star, a friendly innkeeper, a couple unable to find a room – a situation faced by many refugees. There were no baubles or tinsel, only the love of Joseph and Mary and their love for the infant. The child did not shine or have extraordinary powers but merely nestled in his mother's breast. Shepherds came in nervously, not quite sure why they were there, and knelt in the straw to gaze at the baby while cow and donkey looked on. It was all so ordinary, so simple. Such events happen every day in our world.

But there was another world in the picture or, rather, a mysterious part of our world that we never normally notice. There was a mystery about this event that waited to be enjoyed. Angels, God's messengers, broke into the scene, singing 'Glory'. The child looked like any other but he was the Son of God. Mysteries like this cannot be solved but they can be savoured. In the Christ child – 'Word made flesh' – we see simplicity and great mystery brought together.

To have simplicity without mystery is to experience only half of our world. It is like looking at a negative of a photograph when we could have a full-colour print. It is to miss out on the richness and depth of our world. It is to lose out on the joy of wonder and the feeling of awe. There is much in our world that our minds will never comprehend but which our hearts can grasp. The true Christmas will always contain simplicity and mystery.

CHRISTMAS AND THE SOLSTICE

We do not know when the Christ was born but there is need to celebrate the occasion and to fix a festival. Without predetermined dates, memories fade and the story would not be told. There is need for set times and places if our faith is to be anchored and our love shown. Dates should not be just random but chosen as much as possible to indicate what the festival is about and to move its purpose forward. The date chosen to celebrate the coming of Christ is near the winter solstice, when the days are at their shortest. From his coming, light increases and days lengthen. With his appearance, the deep darkness is past and a brighter and longer day is on the way.

In the Hebrides, Christmas Eve is called the 'Long Night'. It is the time when darkness seems to triumph but with Christ's coming the Long Night is past. We rejoice that, in the Christ, new light and life are brought into the world and, through him, our days and our whole lives increase. For many, the tradition is to meet at midnight and to celebrate the coming of the Lord of Light.

At the opposite side of the year, we celebrate the summer solstice and, near that, we have the festival of the birth of St John the Baptist on 24 June. From this day, the light decreases until the winter solstice and Christmas. These two festivals were chosen with great thought to express not only the coming of light and life in the Christ, but also to remember the words of the Baptist concerning Jesus: 'He must increase but I must decrease.'

There is a lovely thought concerning the end of the Long Night from the people of the Hebrides. They believe that when the Christ comes the sea, the sky, the earth and all creatures glow with his light.

THE LONG NIGHT

This is the long night
We wait for the light
Ho Ri,* Ho Ri, blessed is he
This is the cold time
Before the joy of dawn
Before the coming of God
Ho Ri, Ho Ri, blessed is he
His birth on Christmas morn
Christ without beginning or end
He comes as our eternal friend
Ho Ri, Ho Ri, blessed is he
Son of the dawn, Son of the sky
Son of earth, God most high
Son of God, Son of man
Sharing with us God's plan
Ho Ri, Ho Ri, blessed is he
Tonight the earth is bright
Sea and shore shine with light
Shine for him hill and earth
Shine for him heart and hearth
Ho Ri, Ho Ri, blessed is he
Rejoice, he comes to set us free
To let us share in eternity
Ho Ri, Ho Ri, blessed is he

* From the Gaelic, meaning 'Hail to the King'

To Lila from
Robert Buhler

THE WONDER OF MARY

My child a mere breath
And yet the breath of God
Of my flesh and blood
And the Divine Love
A limited edition
Yet from eternity
Frail, fragile flesh
Filled with the Almighty
Belonging to heaven
Yet born on earth
Possessing nothing
Though Lord of all
Created out of love
And for my love
God is with you
My little child

A CHANGING SCENE

The brown-green hillside of last night
Had been transformed!
Before first light a determined army
Had silently blanketed every bit of ground
The snow, untouched, unsullied
Was pure delight
Soon it became
Like the background to a vivid painting
Brilliant colour was added
Scarves, bright coats, and hats
And movement, with whizzing sledges
Snowballs fights and the building
Of the jolliest snowman
Family after family descended on the field
At its busiest since this time last year

THE CHURCH OF THE NATIVITY

I come inside with awe
Cap held in my hand
To bow before the infant
Looking at the Christ child
I worship with the shepherds
I hear the of Word made flesh
And know the love of God
I sing 'Glory' with the angels
Praying for peace on earth
And goodwill among all people
I offer my gift to the infant King
With the Magi and hope that
It is as meaningful as theirs
I receive the living Lord
I hold him in my hands
I am filled with wonder and awe
Then I go on my way rejoicing
Glorifying and praising God

TO BEGIN THE NEW

Stand still in silence
And the sound you will hear
Across the frosty, starlit air
Is the song of the midnight bell
Ushering in another year

Open your door and heart in welcome
And share your food and drink
Showing kind hospitality
To your friend and to the stranger
Pattern for another year

Look forward in faith
And seek to chase away fear
Rejoice that God is with you
(Whatever may suddenly appear)
And welcome in another year

Set sins and sorrows behind you
The past year is over and gone
Seek and find new confidence
As you begin to journey on
And celebrate the New Year

THE NEW WISE MEN

Like the Magi they travelled far
And yet they hardly left the room
They probed deep mysteries
For meaning and purpose
Saw new stars dancing, galaxies being born
And entered into the depths of the unknown

Those explorers of the microcosm
Watching the whirl of creation
Tracing life back to its source
In the spiral of human DNA
Their voyages, like the Magi's,
Will reshape our world
Alter all our relationships
And change us for ever

WINTER AS A TIME FOR REST

Winter is when certain animals hibernate and will not be seen until the spring. The grass and trees have a time of rest, expending less energy. In the old calendars and in the Book of Hours, winter was shown as a time for being at home. It was a time for closing the door and sitting in front of the fire. It was a time to rejoice in the shelter of our homes and the love of our families. This was the time for story and for reflection. It was a time to slow down and conserve our energies. Winter was seen as a balance to the hectic life of summer, when we were out of doors and active, perhaps even hyperactive.

Winter calls us to recognize the need for withdrawal, for rest and reflection. It is a call for us to discover that we are not separate from nature. Sadly, we are in danger of making winter as busy, if not busier, than summer. With modern heating and travel, we are able to venture far from home. We fight against the elements and feel we ought to be able to control them. We believe that nothing should stop for very long. The build up to Christmas and the January sales are signs of our unrest. We are coerced into busyness and enticed to want more and more. It is not surprising that many find winter exhausting.

Seek to make some space in each day to rest and to reflect. Celebrate the ability to be able to stop. People without breaks are as dangerous as cars without brakes. Work is better done if we can be relaxed and at ease. Make room for the people you live with and the people you work with. Spend some time enjoying their presence and sharing their stories. With all our modern means of communication, we are at risk of no longer taking our time to listen to each other. This winter celebrate the relationships you have and spend some time each day enjoying them.

FROZEN PEOPLE

He was unmoved by the beauty
Unresponsive to the challenge
He told me the kind of things he didn't do
I wanted to know what he had done!
He was negative towards life
Seemingly indifferent to joy
Can we really give thanks
For those who are not tempted?
Surely no life can be so dull
Warm blood must race
And pulsate in everyone's veins
Hearts must beat and throb
To the thrill and joy of life
Not to risk or venture forth
Is to stagnate and die
I pray for the frozen people
For those with fixed attitudes
And closed minds

LIFE IS MEANT TO THRILL

The ski-master did not seem to be very impressive in the hotel. He was never seen to hurry. He did not seem anxious to get going. He was not a young man and it looked as if he found walking a little painful. Yet once he was on the slopes he was amazing, bounding with energy and with superb control. His words have stayed with me and have been a source of guidance:

'If you are unwilling to make the uphill journey and to struggle against the elements, you will never enjoy the thrill and freedom of the downhill return.

'The great art is to relax. So many things are not possible if you cannot approach them in a relaxed manner. You will not be able to ski if your body is tense. To be too rigid will result in a fall. There is a great art in learning to let yourself go. Take your time and make sure your whole body is at ease. Learn to wind down so that your energies can be used where they are needed. Then you can focus on where you are going.

'If you are afraid of a few falls, you may as well hang up your skis. No one has achieved much without making mistakes. Those who extend themselves and stretch their horizons will have a few tumbles and setbacks. You can learn from your falls – and you can rise from them.

'If you are worried about people laughing at you, you will get nowhere. Such worry has stopped many a person beginning. Most achievers were once awkward on the slopes. Those who know what it is to learn and to try will not laugh at you, although they may laugh with you.

'Get out there and extend yourself. You cannot imagine the freedom you will have or get it from books. No one can describe to you the thrill that is yours when you use your life to the full. To know life, you have to live it and know that life is meant to thrill.'

CANDLEMAS

We begin in the dark
Like much of our lives
Then there was a spark
A dancing lick of flame
Lighting a large candle
Words rang around us:
'The light of Christ.'
The darkness diminishes
And in unison we reply:
'Thanks be to God.'
Many candles are now lit
Light is stronger than darkness
We each hold a candle
Flooding the church with light
'The Lord is my light
And he is my salvation.'
The forty days of Christmas
Have climaxed in light
Lord of light eternal, shine
In our hearts and in our lives

The feast of the Presentation of Christ in the Temple on 2 February is forty days after Christmas and rounds off the Christmas season. It is known as Candlemas from the tradition of lighting many candles for this celebration.

THE MIRACLE OF LIFE

The winter struggles on
Frost and cold keep hold
Yet the snowdrops are up
And colour is in the willow
Catkins hang with icicles
But the earth is turning green
The celandine are through
And lambs call in the field
New life waits to show itself
The sap has begun to rise
Almost the end of winter
And spring of another year

THE ACONITES

The wood was dark and cold
Brown leaves and snow afoot
All felt dull and even lifeless
Until I saw the seam of gold

Bursting brightly from the earth
Enriching me and all who'd see
The aconites braving the frost
Enduring the light snow

Sages travelled far seeking a star
Looking for light and new life
I shout with joy, 'I've found it
in the golden glowing aconite.'

Before the bud turns into leaf
Before the birds begin to sing
Here is the precious aconite
Bright harbinger of spring

WINTER IS OVER

Frogs sing in unfrozen ponds
Spawn replacing sheets of ice
Hedges suggest a hint of green
Buds like candles deck the trees
Celandine and daffodil appear
Blossom is upon the cherry tree
Sparrows enjoy choosing a mate
Woodpecker drumming fills the air
Robin, in song, declares his territory
Wild bees are working so busily
Sun has warmed their winter tomb
Winter dead, butterflies appear
There's a resurrection in the air
Touching tree, animal and flower
Saying to us: 'Lo, the winter is past.'
Days are lengthened, life extends
I am able to walk out after tea
Seven daisies I cover with a hand
Folklore tells me winter is over

C Neal

ILLUSTRATIONS